Y0-CUW-157

Cathy's Candles

Cathy's Candles

Rekindle an Old Craft—
Create Candles
by Reusing & Recycling

Catherine Basten

Universal Publishers
Boca Raton, Florida

*Cathy's Candles: Rekindle an Old Craft--
Create Candles by Reusing and Recycling*

Copyright © 2004 Catherine Basten
All rights reserved.

Universal Publishers/uPUBLISH.com
Boca Raton, Florida
USA • 2004

ISBN: 1-58112-543-7

To my husband, Gene,
for all your help in seeking items that could be recycled for molds, but mostly for your talent in making iron candleholders that enhance the beauty of my finished candles.

To our daughter, Sara,
Thank you for participating and showing willingness in rekindling the art of candle making.

To our son, Robert,
Thank You for your encouraging statement: "Mom, go for it!"

To our son, Patrick,
Thank you for your patience in sharing your computer assistance and knowledge. Without your expertise *Cathy's Candles* would not be a reality!

Contents

Candle Poem 3
Introduction 4
Equipment & Supplies 7
Notes 17
Dipped Candles 19
Antique Dipped Candles 24
Tube Candles 28
Votive Candles 31
Cranberry and Citrus Votive 34
Clay Pot Candles 37
Antique Coated Votive Candles 40
Antique Muffin Tin Candles 44
Antique Candy Mold Ornament 48
Carved Candles 50
Antique Cookie Cutter Candle 54
Floating Candle 57
Cinnamon Rectangle Candle 61
Antique Rectangle Candle 65
Square Candles 69
Candles Made From Old Tins 72
Variable Candle 76
Container Candles 80
Cylinder Candles 83
Beeswax Cinnamon Stick Candle 87
Whipped Candle 90

Cinnamon Apple Candle 94
Oatmeal and Honey Candle................................. 97
Egg Shaped Candle 100
Pinecone Fire Starters..103
Lemon Citronella Candle 106
Bowl Candles..109
Luminaries..112
Fruit Candleholder...116
Frequently Asked Questions 118

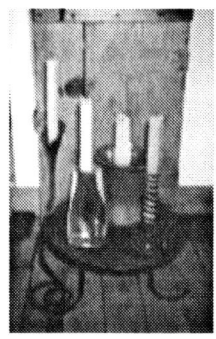

Candle Poem

A candle's but a simple thing,
It starts with just a bit of string.
Yet dipped and dipped with patient hand,
It gathers wax upon the strand.
Until, complete and snowy white,
It fires at last a lovely light.
Life seems so like that bit of string;
Each deed we do a simple thing.
Yet day-by-day if on life's strand
We work with patient heart and hand
It gathers joy, makes dark days bright,
And gives at last... a lovely light.

      --Author Unknown

Introduction

I would like to share with you my love in the art of "Candle making". Through *Cathy's Candles* book any novice can begin to make candles with ease and confidence. In a short period of time after using these instructions you will feel like an expert candle maker. If you create a candle that you just can't live with, then re-melt the wax, and begin your project again. That is the beauty of "Candle making"!

Candle making should not only be a fun experience, but an experience that will give you hours of enjoyment. A candle made with your favorite soothing scent is a relaxing and satisfying form of aromatherapy for whatever ails you!

My favorite place to work and create candles is "Up North" in the great State of Minnesota. Minnesota's natural beauty and serenity that surrounds us is what puts me in an instant creative mode.

Candles make a wonderful gift that can be used for all occasions. You just have to be a little creative and add personality to each candle idea. I have learned to improvise on what can be used as molds for my candles. Some ideas are: plastic cups, paper cups, salmon cans, tuna cans, cardboard potato chip container, and anything else I can find at home or in a grocery store that can later be used for a mold. When it comes to making container candles my ideas keep flowing: half pint canning jars, different and unique glasses, coffee mugs, and just about anything that I can get my hands on. Garage sales, flea markets, or the GOODWILL store are great places to purchase molds, containers, or melting pans. The woods are full of natural additives for my candles, grapevines to add that natural look rapped around your candle, or rose hips and dried flowers to create that country look. Just look around and utilize whatever you find from our many earth's treasures.

When it comes to candleholders that is where my husband's help comes in handy. Gene will cut a block from a tree, or carve a piece of willow for a natural candleholder. He will also make candleholders for me from metal or rod iron, shaping and welding them creating a unique design. Let your imagination flow and utilize glass bottles, old threading spools, and even old muffin tins for candleholders.

Art and crafts have been a large part of my life, but mainly I like to do creations that can be made from discarded or natural items. Of course, candle making will always be a fun part of my life. You will find yourself looking at other candles in a different way. Wondering how that candle is made, what to display that candle on, and finally what can I utilize for a mold. Let your imagination and creative instincts go with you. Remember when you look for a container for a candle gift; match it with that person's style or personality. But mostly, enjoy a moment of burning a favorite candle.

Good luck with your adventure into "Candle Making"!

Equipment and Supplies

Wax is very flammable, and never should be unattended during the melting process. All projects should be done only with adult supervision. Protective gear should be worn, eye protection to prevent injuries in case of wax spurting, apron to protect clothing, rubber gloves during dipping candles to prevent any burn that occur, and mostly shoes warn in case of any wax that might spill down on you or the floor. Always safety first with common sense used during candle dipping. This will insure a more successful candle and a more pleasant experience.

Next we need a container for melting the wax or paraffin. They're a lot of options on cans that can be used for melting the wax into, an 11.5 oz. Coffee, a large spaghetti sauce can, or a large can from peanut butter. The important thing is to remember the size of the can you use will determine the amount of wax you will melt. This can is used to hold your wax chunks that will be melted for your project. Prepare your melting can by pinching a pouring spout so that the melted wax will pour out at a slower pace. Again I cannot impress the importance of care and safety when pouring hot melted wax. Wax can cause burns so use all the precautions needed to protect you from injury. You will place the melting can into water to aid in the melting process. You will need at least several inches of water on the bottom of your double boiler or electric frying at all times. The water will evaporate during the heating process so always monitor your water level in your pan and add more water when needed.

Crock pot– for melting wax. A crock-pot can be used to melt your wax. This enables the wax to melt at a low temperature.

Double boiler pans or an **electric frying pan**- is used to heat the wax. I prefer to use the electric frying pan because you can control the temperature easier. I like to keep my wax melting between 130 – 150 degrees. Wax is very flammable, so temperature control is a must. Never heat wax directly in a pan that you have placed on a burner, because the wax will start on fire! When you use a double boiler you will need a wax thermometer to control the melting temperature, and heat at a low temperature.

Molds– during my different projects I will talk about many different household items to use as molds.

Some of these items that can be used are: milk cartons, salmon cans, Dixie cups, plastic cups, 1" metal pipe, tomato cans, frozen juice containers, potato chip cylinder containers, and oatmeal containers. Just use your imagination and look around the house for various ideas. If you are using a plastic or metal mold you will need to prepare the mold with coating the inside lightly with any vegetable oil or silicone spray. This will aid the candle in separating from the mold easier. While looking for cans to use, keep in mind that they can't have ridges inside. Ridges on cans may prevent you from removing the candle from the mold; therefore you may need to use a can with a smooth wall inside. The molds bottom needs to be the same size as the top so the candle can be removed from the mold after the wax sets up fully. Candy molds and muffin tins are needed for molds on some of my projects.

Dixie cups– for storing the excess candle wax. The next time you begin a project just tear off the paper of the Dixie cup and reuse the wax for melting. A Dixie cup can be used as a mold also.

Wax Thermometer– is used to control the temperature during melting. Wax should generally be melted between 130 degrees – 150 degrees.

Mold Seal or putty- is used to seal around a mold or a piece of pipe to prevent the wax from escaping.

Wicks– are available on the Internet on candle supplier's sites, and at your local craft center. There are various types of wicks available. Follow the manufacture instructions on what size to use according to the diameter of the candle. You will have to prepare your wick before the final insertion. To prepare your wicks soak the wick into the melted wax for about five minutes and remove the wick to dry. Cut your wick ¼ inch higher than your candle.

Stearine – this is an additive used to help the wax from shrinking so that the wax will become easier to release when making molded candles, and also helps slow the wax from dripping during the burning process. Stearine also makes the wax translucent, and adds an opaque look. When the wax is melted it lowers the melting point and when the wax cools this makes the candle harder in order to prevent bending or slumping. Stearine should be melted prior to adding candle wax. Follow the manufacture instructions on how much to use per pound. (Caution: use Stearine with paraffin wax not beeswax. It should never be used with rubber mold materials, because it acts as a caustic.)

Candle scent– this can also be purchased at a craft store or on the Internet from a candle-making supplier. You can buy this in a liquid form or small blocks. I prefer the liquid form. Follow the manufacture instructions on how much to use.

Candle dyes come in small blocks. Use a small shaving of the candle dye first, and then add more as you feel the need. To test the color you have produced, spoon a small amount of the colored wax unto a piece of wax paper. If this is not the desired color then add more dye to the melted wax. Repeat this process until you create that perfect color for your candle. Remember denser the wax is the more dense the color will become. You can use crayons for coloring, but because of the oil used in crayons they will produce a molted look on the candle.

Knife – is used for cutting the wax blocks into small chunks. The smaller the chunks the quicker the wax will melt. Keep this knife only for this project. The knife should be keep sharpen and remember to use caution when using a sharp knife so you will not cut yourself.

Welding rod or **metal knitting rod**– is used as a wicking rod. The size of the rod should be as close to the diameter of your wick. My husband made a handle at the top of my rod to protect me from puncturing my hand while pressing down on the rod.

Scale- is used for measuring your wax. It is very important to measure the amount of wax needed to add the correct amount of Stearine, dyes, or scent. Weight one pound of wax, chunk the wax into small pieces, and then melt it in your pan. Make a mark where the line is for one pound of melted wax. Continue this for marking two pounds or however much melted wax can be held into your can. Use the pound marks for your next project.

Beeswax – is a natural product that should be used with candle wax. I like to melt half beeswax and half candle wax. This formula is used because beeswax has a tendency to burn very quickly and spurts while the candle is burning. Beeswax can be purchased at suppliers that handle candle-making supplies, but I prefer to find a local beekeeper and purchase my beeswax directly from him. Sometime beekeepers advertise beeswax for sale in your local paper.

Candle wax - comes in a large block or chunks. This can be purchased on the net or at your craft store. Candle wax has some Stearine already in the wax to help the wax harden. Remember; never leave your melting wax unattended. Always keep your fire extinguisher handy just in case of the melting wax catching on fire. Safety first! Children without adult supervision should never do these projects unattended!

Paraffin Wax – can be used for candle making. You can purchase this wax from a grocery store in the canning department, or you can purchase candle wax in a large block or chunks at your local craft store. Remember; never leave your melting wax unattended. Keep a fire extinguisher handy when working with melting wax. Safety first! Children without adult supervision should never do these projects unattended!

Tallow candles– candles can be made from tallow (rendered animal fat). After you render the fat add ½ lb of alum and ½ lb of salt pepper per lb of fat. These additives aid in the hardening of the candle. Beef fat is preferred over sheep fat.

Old baking pan – can be used to pour melted wax into for rolling candles to give it an antique look. Garage sales are good places to find old equipment that is needed for candle making. This pan should only be used for your candle making.

Spoon or dowel - is used to mix the scent or stir the color. Put these aside and only use for your candle making projects.

Wicks – can be made from cotton string. The string will need to be prepared by adding one part salt, two parts borax, to 10 parts water. Soak the string into the solution for 8- 12 hours and then let dry. I have not had much success with homemade wicks.

Herbal scents – powdered or dried herbs can be used to scent wax. You can strain the herbs from the melted wax by using cheesecloth over a pan and slowly pour the melted wax into the pan. Or you can keep the dried herbs in the melted wax to give it a more natural appearance. If you do decide to keep the dried herbs in you wax, remember as the wax melts the dried herbs can create a burnt aroma instead of your pleasant scent that you had originally intended. Do not leave your candle that has dried herbs or flowers in the wax burn completely down, because the dried flower or herb can start on fire!

Candle care – to give your candle a lustrous shine you can just rub the outside of the candle with oil. For an old or dirty candle you can rub gently on the outside of the candle with an old nylon to give the candle a shinier look. Always make sure that you burn your candle in an area that cannot catch anything on fire. Also make sure your candles are securely place on any candleholder. A protection covering placed under your candle is a must! This will protect your furniture from being ruined from melted wax dripping down on it. If you want your candle to burn longer you can put the candle in the freezer for 5 minutes. Chilling the candle will slow down the burning process. When your candle looses it scent you can just sprinkle a small amount of scent on your candle to revive its scent. Beeswax candles have a tendency to bloom (your candle will have a cloudy low luster appearance). Take a nylon stocking or piece of nylon and rub the candle lightly. Watch the candles regain that lustrous shine again.

Notes:

You can straighten your tapered candles by heating the candle slowly with a blow dryer and then roll the candle on a flat surface. This method works well with removing any outer bubbles that have occurred on the tapered candle during the dipping process. If your container candle looses it scent, light the candle and when it has a small poll of melted wax add a small amount of scent into the melted wax.

Always keep your candles stored in a dry area out of the direct sun. Years ago they stored their candles in a wooden box to enable the candle to breathe. I wrap individual candles in tissue paper for stacking, and lay my dipped candles flat to keep their shape.

Cleaning wax off clothing is very simple. Let the wax set up fully and scrap off as much as you can. If this doesn't seem to come off then put the piece of clothing in the freezer to set the wax up fully and then scrap the wax off. If any oil resin is let on the clothing, place a piece of brown bag on top of the affect area with a warm iron to remove the wax. You may have to do this several times using a clean piece of brown bag each time. Add spot cleaner on the oil spot and launder as usual.

If wax falls on the floor wait until it sets up and scrap the wax away with a plastic spatula. Remember it is very important to prepare the area that you use to make candles with to help prevent any damage to your countertop or floor.

Dipped Candles:

Supplies needed:

- ✓ Candle wax / beeswax half pound of each) or
- ✓ Candle wax (one pound)
- ✓ Prepared wick
- ✓ A double boiler used for melting wax, and a tall jar or can for dipping your candles into. I use a large olive jar for dipping the candles because it is tall. Whatever jar you use to dip the candle it should be taller than the height of your dipped candle
- ✓ Candle dyes/beeswax has its own natural color
- ✓ Candle scent/beeswax has its own natural scent

Please see the equipment and supply page for further instructions on how to prepare your wicks, how much candle scent or dye to use, what type of dipping jar to use, and other tips you will need to know before you begin your project.

First melt the candle wax in a pan with the dipping jar placed into the center of the water at a low temperature. A double boiler works well with this project because you can hold more water for melting the jar of was that is used for dipping. There should be about one to two inches of water at all times. When I make beeswax candles I like to use half candle wax and half beeswax. Pure beeswax candles burn very fast and will spurt as they burn. Always be conscious about adding water because it will evaporate away. Never leave wax unattended during melting time, as it is very flammable! Next you will want to prepare your wicks by soaking them into the melted wax for about 5 minutes. Now take the wicks out of the dipped candles wax, straighten the wicks and place them onto a piece of wax paper to dry.

When wax is melted completely add the dyes. A tip to check the color is to drop some colored wax on a wax paper to check if this is the shade that you desire. Beeswax candles have their own natural color and scent to them, so you do not need to add any scent or dye to the wax. Then gently stir the wax mixture. The pan should be kept at a low temperature. When making straight candle wax candles add your scent after the wax is completely melted.

Now the dipping process begins. Cut your wick about 1 inch longer than the height you want your candle to be. Dip the wick into the wax slowly just adding a layer of wax then quickly bring the wick out of the jar. You will continue this process one dip at a time. After several dips I like to cool the wax into a jar of cold water. Dipping the wick into the jar quickly and gently wiping any water off the wick (or future candle). This seems to help the candle except the added layers of wax quicker. Through this process of continual dipping the candle will seem to form a curve shape. Don't worry you can remedy this by rolling the candle gently on a hard surface making the candle straighter. Also after your candle has been dipped several times it will form a drip on the bottom. At this time I cut the drip off the end keeping the length consistent.

Sometimes beads will form on the outer layer of the candle. These beads are caused from dipping the candles into the water for the cooling process. To remove the beads from the candle's outer layer, while the candle is still warm, just gently roll the candle on a hard surface. This procedure works well, and you may have to do this several times before you have finished the last layer of dipping.

You can dip two candles at a time by cutting the wick twice as long and folding the wick over in half. If you really want to be productive you can make a dipping holder out of a piece of wood. (Approximate size of 2 inch by 5 inch) This piece of wood should have slots grooved symmetrically about one inch apart on each side. This grove will aid as a place to secure the wick from moving while you dip your candles. For this size of a holder I would only put four slots on each side. Remember if you are using this type of an holder, you will have accommodate the size of the jar or can to dip the candles into The wicks will need to be cut long enough to fit across to the next grove and still maintain the desired length.

There are so many different candleholders that work well with dipped candles. I use pottery vases, antique spool, cast iron candleholder, unique glass bottles, and various shapes of driftwood. If you have the tools available, drilling a hole in the center of a favorite rock makes an interesting candleholder. My husband makes candleholders out of cutting a block from a tree branch, and drilling a hole in the center for the candle. Use your imagination and you probably can find ideas right around your home.

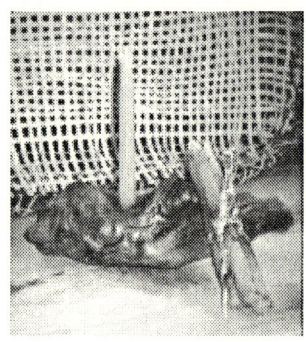

Antique Dipped Candles

Supplies needed:
- ✓ Candle wax/ Beeswax (one pound of each)
- ✓ Prepared wicks
- ✓ Ground cinnamon
- ✓ Candle dye (if making from candle wax/beeswax has its own natural color)
- ✓ Candle scent (if making from candle wax/beeswax has its own natural scent)
- ✓ A double boiler used for melting wax, and a tall jar or can for dipping your candles into. The jar should be taller than the height of your finished candle.

Please see the equipment and supply page for further instructions on how to prepare your wicks, how much candle dye and scent to use, what type of jar to use for dipping, and other tips you will need to know before you begin your project.

First melt the candle wax in a pan with the dipping jar placed into the center of the water at a low temperature. A double boiler works well with this project because you can hold more water for melting the jar of was that is used for dipping. There should be about one to two inches of water at all times.

When I make beeswax candles I like to use half candle wax and half beeswax. Pure beeswax candles burn very fast and will spurt as they burn. Always be conscious about adding water because it will evaporate away. Never leaving wax unattended during melting time as it is very flammable! Next you will want to prepare your wicks by soaking the wicks into the melted wax for about 5 minutes. Next take the wicks out of the wax, straighten the wicks, and place them onto a piece of wax paper to dry. When wax is melted completely add the dyes. A tip to check the color is to drop some colored wax on a wax paper to check if this is the shade that you desire. Beeswax candles have their own natural color and scent to them, so you do not need to add any scent or dye to the wax. Then gently stir the wax mixture. The pan should be kept at a low temperature.

Now the dipping process begins. Cut your wick about 1 inch longer than the height you want your candle to be. Dip the wick into the wax slowly just adding a layer of wax then quickly bring the wick out of the jar. You will continue this process one dip at a time. After several dips I like to cool the wax into a jar of cold water. Dipping the wick into the jar quickly and gently wiping any water off the wick (or future candle). This seems to help the candle except the added layers of wax quicker. Through this process of continual dipping the candle will seem to form a curve shape. Don't worry you can remedy this by rolling the candle gently on a hard surface making the candle straighter. Also after your candle has been dipped several times it will form a drip on the bottom. At this time I cut the drip off the end keeping the length consistent. Sometimes beads will form on the outer layer of the candle. These beads are caused from dipping the candles into the water for the cooling process. To remove the beads from the candle's outer layer, while the candle is still warm, just gently roll the candle on a hard surface. This procedure works well, and you may have to do this several times before you have finished the last layer of dipping.

You can dip two candles at a time by cutting the wick twice as long and folding the wick over in half. If you really want to be productive you can make a dipping holder out of a piece of wood. (Approximate size of 2 inch by 5 inch) This piece of wood should have slots grooved symmetrically about one inch apart on each side. This grove will aid as a place to secure the wick from moving while you dip your candles. For this size of a holder I would only put four slots on each side. Remember if you are using this type of an holder, you will have accommodate the size of the jar or can to dip the candles into The wicks will need to be cut long enough to fit across to the next grove and still maintain the desired length.

Now you can begin to antique your dipped candle. Melt some candle wax at a low temperature. Add ground cinnamon to the melted wax until it is dark in color. Using a bowl to catch the drippings begin to pour slowly over the dipped candle. Repeat this process several times until you have the look you desire. If there are drips formed on the outside of the candle just roll the candle on a flat surface.

Tube candles

Supplies Needed:
- ✓ 1" or 2" metal plumbing pipe for mold 12" long
- ✓ Silicone spray or vegetable oil
- ✓ Mold seal or putty
- ✓ Stearine
- ✓ Candle wax/Beeswax (one pound will make three candles)
- ✓ Candle scent for candle wax project/beeswax has its own natural scent
- ✓ Candle dye for candle wax project/beeswax has its own natural color
- ✓ Prepared wick
- ✓ Wicking rod (dimension of wick and length needed)
- ✓ Double boiler or electric frying pan and a can for melting wax

Please see the equipment and supply page for further instructions on how to prepare your wicks, what Stearine is used for, whether to use a double boiler or electric frying pan, and other tips you will need to know before you begin your projects.

First melt Stearine at a low temperature. Stearine is used to help the candle separate from the mold.

Then melt the wax at a low temperature around 150 degrees. When I make beeswax candles I use half beeswax and half candle wax. This project can also be made with candle wax adding your favorite scent and dye. Never leave melting wax unattended or without adult supervision. You will need to prepare the wick by soaking the wick into the melted wax for about 5 minutes, and then remove to dry. While the wax is melted you will need to add your candle dye. A tip to check the shade is by dropping some dyed wax onto wax paper. If this is not the shade you want then just add more dye to the wax. Remember the denser the wax the darker the shade! I add the candle scent when the wax is fully melted.

Coat the mold lightly with silicone spray or any vegetable oil. Then place the mold into a mound of putty, this will keep the wax from flowing out and help secure the mold in a vertical position.

Pour the wax into the mold slowly. When the wax is partially set up, it will have a cloudy appearance; insert the rod down the center of the candle making a hole for your wick. When the wax is fully set up remove the candle from the piping by tapping lightly on the pipe. The candle should fall out.

If you have difficulty with the candle coming out of the mold, place the mold in the freezer for about five minutes, and then run under warm water. Again tap lightly on the mold to remove the candle. You will need to insert the wick down the hole after the candle is fully set up.

I like giving these tube candles in-groups of three. The candles above are shown wrapped together with a torn strip of cotton material. This candle, with its slender height, works well with a pottery vase holding the candle.

You may be able to come up with your own idea on what to use as a candleholder for your tube candle.

Votive candles

Supplies needed:
- ✓ Candle wax/Beeswax (one pound)
- ✓ Stearine
- ✓ Prepared wicks
- ✓ Dixie cups (3 oz. or 5 oz.)
- ✓ Candle scent
- ✓ Candle dyes
- ✓ Wicking rod
- ✓ Double boiler or electric frying pan and a can for melting wax

Please see the equipment and supply page for further instructions on how to prepare your wicks, what Stearine is used for, how much candle dye or scent to use, whether to use a double boiler or electric frying pan, and other tips you will need to know before you begin your project.

First melt the correct amount of Stearine at a low temperature. Then place your candle wax chunks in the can and melt at a low temperature.

If you are making a beeswax candle, then melt half beeswax and half candle wax. If you use all beeswax the candle will burn much faster and pure beeswax candles have a tendency to spurt when burnt.

While the wax is melting you may prepare your wicks. You do this by soaking the wick in the melted wax for five minutes. After soaking remove and dry. Add you candle dye to the melting wax. A tip to check the shade is by dropping some dyed wax on wax paper. If this is not the shade you want then just add more dye to the wax. Remember the denser the wax the darker the shade

When the wax is completely melted slowly pour the wax into the Dixie cup. After the wax is partially set up, insert the wicking rod down the center of the candle for later placement of the wick. The wax at this point will look cloudy and have a thicker appearance.

Sometimes when the candle hardens the center of the candle will appear a dip. Don't worry; this can be remedied easily by filling in more melted wax to fill in that area.

Remove the Dixie cup from the wax when it is fully set up and hard. Now you may insert your prepared wick into the hole that you have made.

A votive candle can be used with many styles of candleholders, half pint canning jar, juice glass, pottery plate, or a pint-canning jar with sand on the bottom. I am always scouting for unique jars or pieces of pottery that I can later use with all my different styles and sizes of candles. Look in those cupboards and you may just find that right candleholder that you need for your candle.

Cranberry and Citrus Votive

Supplies needed:
- ✓ Candle wax (one pound)
- ✓ Stearine
- ✓ Wicking rod
- ✓ Prepared candlewick
- ✓ Double boiler or electric frying pan and a can for melting wax
- ✓ Candle scents/cranberry and citrus
- ✓ Candle dyes/red and yellow
- ✓ Dried fruit or herbs/dried cranberries and dried oranges
- ✓ Molds: Dixie cups 3oz

Please see the equipment and supply page for further instructions on how to prepare your wicks, what Stearine is used for, how much candle dye and scent to use, whether to use a double boiler or electric frying

pan, and other tips you will need to know before you begin your project.

First melt the Stearine in a pan at a low temperature. Next melt your wax at a low temperature. Never leave your melting wax unattended! Wax is very flammable!

When the wax is melted completely, add the candle dye slowly in order to acquire the shade you want. A tip to check the shade is by dropping some dyed wax on wax paper. If this is not the shade you want then just add more dye to the wax. Then gently stir the melted wax. While the wax is melting you may prepare your wicks. To prepare your wicks you soak the wick in the melted wax for five minutes. Remove the wicks to dry.

When the wax is fully melted pour the wax into your 3 oz. Dixie cups. Set aside some of your dyed waxes in case you need to fill in any shrinkage areas.

After the wax is partially set up, prepare the hole for your wick. Push the wicking rod down the center of the wax, and then insert the prepared wick into that hole. Allow the wax to fully set up before removing from the Dixie cup. Sometimes the wax will shrink and leave a dip in the center of the candle. Just melt some more wax and fill in that area.

Follow these instructions for both candles:
Place the votive candle in a small juice glass or half-pint canning jar. Add your dried fruit around your votive candle. Now your candle arrangement is complete.

Please keep in mind that whenever you add anything dried to your candle, caution and common sense should always be used. Never leave the wax burn all the way down, or it will start the dried herbs on fire. Safety with burning candles is a MUST!

Clay Pot Candles

Supplies needed:
- ✓ Any size clay pot for candleholder
- ✓ Candle wax (one pound)
- ✓ Dixie cups (3 oz. or 5 oz.)
- ✓ Candle scent/red and yellow
- ✓ Candle scent/cranberry and citrus
- ✓ Prepared wicks
- ✓ Wicking rod
- ✓ Stearine
- ✓ Double boiler or electric frying pan and a can to melt wax

Please see the equipment and supply page for further instructions on how to prepare your wicks, what Stearine is used for, whether to use a double boiler or

electric frying pan, and other tips you will need to know before you begin your project.

First you will need to decide what type of clay pot candle you will be making. You can set a votive candle inside the clay pot or pour the wax into the clay pot. Either type of clay pot candle you will need to make sure that the hole on the bottom is sealed with putty or wax. Another idea is to fill the clay pot with sand to hold a tube candle.

To make a candle in clay pot, melt your Stearine first at a low temperature. Next add your wax chunks and melt them at a low temperature. While the wax is melting add your candle dye. A tip to check the shade is by dropping some dyed wax onto wax paper. If this is not the shade you want then just add more dye to the wax.

To prepare your wicks soak the wick into the melted wax for five minutes and remove to dry.

After the wax is fully melted add your candle scent. Stir the scent in the wax gently. Now pour the wax into your clay pot slowly. A dip might appear in the center of your candle during the cooling stage. If this happens just add more melted wax and fill in that area.

When the wax is partially set up insert the wicking rod down the center of the candle for your wick. The wax will appear cloudy. Insert the wick in the hole that you have made after the wax is fully set up.

Antique Coated Votive Candles

Supplies needed:
- ✓ Candle wax/ beeswax (one pound) or
- ✓ Candle wax (one pound)
- ✓ Stearine
- ✓ Prepared wicks
- ✓ Dixie cups (3 oz. or 5 oz)
- ✓ Double boiler or electric frying pan and a can for melting wax
- ✓ Candle dyes
- ✓ Candle scents
- ✓ Wicking rod
- ✓ Ground cinnamon
- ✓ Bowl for wax drippings

Please see the equipment and supply page for further instructions on how to prepare your wicks, what

Stearine is used for, whether to use a double boiler or electric frying pan, how much candle dye or scent to use, and other tips you will need to know before you begin your project.

First you will need to make your votive candle before you can antique the candle. Melt the Stearine in your pan at a low temperature. Stearine is used to help the candle separate from the mold. After the Stearine is melted you can begin to add your chunks of candle wax. If you decide to make beeswax candles you will need to mix one/half candle wax with one/half beeswax. Always use a low temperature to melt your wax. Never leave the wax unattended during the melting stage, because wax is very flammable.

Now you will need to prepare your wicks for later insertion. To prepare your wicks soak the wicks into the melted wax for about 5 minutes. After the wicks are fully soaked take them out of the melted wax and lay them on wax paper to dry. During the melting stage you will add your candle dye to the wax. If you are making beeswax candles you will not need to add any dye or scent to your beeswax. Beeswax candles have there own natural color and scent. A tip to check the shade is by dropping some dyed wax on wax paper. If this isn't the right shade you intended then just add more dye to the wax. Remember to keep in mind that the thicker the wax layers the denser the shade will become. When the wax is fully melted add your scent. Pour your melted wax into your Dixie cups. By pouring the wax slowly into the mold it may prevent some air bubbles from forming. After the wax is partially set up, you may insert the wicking rod down the center of the candle. This will make your hole for the wick to be placed later. Allow the wax to harden, and then remove the Dixie cup from the candle. You have made your base votive candle that you will antique. Do not insert your wick into your hole until you have finished the antique layer to your candle.

Melt more candle wax at a low temperature. When the wax is fully melted add your ground cinnamon to the candle wax. This will give the candle an antique appearance. Stir the ground cinnamon gently into the wax, and quickly begin to dip your votive candle into the mixture. An easier way to grip onto the candle while you are pouring the mixture over the candle is to insert your wicking rod into you whole. Pour the melting cinnamon wax over your votive allowing the extra to drip into the bowl. Do this several times to give a thick layer around the votive candle. A tip to smooth out drips on your candle is to roll the candle on a flat surface. Sprinkle some ground cinnamon directly on your candle and then pour more wax over the candle. This will give your candle an uneven dark shade for a more realistic antique appearance. When you are done with pouring the layers on the candle, carve any outer layer of wax off the top of your votive. Doing this you will be able to see the color of the base candle.

I like to display these candles in an old muffin tin. Set one votive in each compartment. Keep your eye out for old muffin tins at Flea Markets or garage sales. Cut your muffin tin in quarters or half so you will only need to set four or six votive candles with a tin.

Antique Muffin Tin Candles

Supplies needed:
- ✓ Candle wax/ beeswax (half pound each) or
- ✓ Candle wax (one pound)
- ✓ Stearine (not to be used with beeswax)
- ✓ Prepared wicks
- ✓ Old muffin tins for mold or using as candleholder
- ✓ Double boiler or electric frying pan and a can for melting wax into
- ✓ Candle dyes (beeswax has its own natural color/ blue for candle wax)
- ✓ Candle scent (beeswax has its own natural scent/ blueberry for candle wax)
- ✓ Wicking rod
- ✓ Double boiler or electric frying pan and a can for melting wax

Please see the equipment and supply page for further instructions on how to prepare your wicks, how much candle dye and scent to use, what Stearine is used for, whether to use a double boiler or electric frying pan, and other tips you will need to know before you begin your project.

First melt the Stearine in your pan before you place your chunks of wax. Stearine is used to help the candle separate from the mold. If you are going burn the candle in the muffin tin then you will not need to do this step of melting Stearine.

Next melt the candle wax at a low temperature. If you are going to use beeswax, then I add half beeswax and half candle wax. Now you will prepare your wicks. Soak the wicks into the melted wax for about 5 minutes, and then remove the wicks from the wax to dry.

While the wax is melting add your candle dye. A tip to check the shade is by dropping some dyed wax onto wax paper. If this isn't the right shade you intended then just add more dye to the wax. Remember to keep in mind that the denser the wax the denser the shade will become. If you are going to do a beeswax candle then you will not need to add any scent or dye. Beeswax has its own natural scent and color. When the wax is fully melted remove the wax from you pan and add your scent.

If you are using the muffin tin for as a mold then you will need to prepare your mold. Coat your mold with vegetable oil. This will help your candle separate from the mold. Whenever using old muffin tins you will need to clean any rust of the tin. It is not necessary to coat your muffin tin if this is going to be used as a candleholder.

After the wax is completely melted pour the wax into the mold slowly. By pouring the wax slowly into the mold this will help prevent air bubbles from forming. After the wax is partially set up, you may insert the wicking rod down the center of the wax in each candle. This is where your wicks will be placed later.

Sometimes when the candle hardens in the center of the wax will appear a dip. Don't worry; this can be remedied easily by filling in more melted wax into that area. That is why I keep a small amount of the dyed wax set aside. You will need to do this for either type of candle.

If you are making the molded candles, when the wax is fully set up you may remove the candles from the molds. To do this just flip the molds upside down and lightly tap the bottom of the mold. The candle should fall out with ease. If this doesn't happen then place the mold into the freezer for about five minutes to help the wax shrink from the mold. Do not leave the candle in the freezer too long or it will begin to crack the wax. After removing the candles from the molds you may insert the prepared wicks.

I have found old muffin tins at flea markets, garage sales, and the Goodwill store. The candle that you made from the muffin tin mold works well as a floating candle.

Antique Candy Mold Ornament

Supplies needed:
- ✓ Candle wax/beeswax
- ✓ Antique candy mold or any candy mold
- ✓ Double boiler or electric frying pan and a can to melt wax

Please see the equipment and supply page for further instructions on what Stearine is used for, whether to use a double boiler or electric frying pan, and other tips you will need to know before you begin your project.

Prepare you mold by lightly coating the inside with vegetable oil. Seal the sides of the mold with wax that has been partially set up so that you can mold the wax around the corners to seal the mold.

Melt half beeswax and half candle wax at a low temperature. When making beeswax projects you do not need to add scent or dye to your wax. Beeswax has its own natural scent and dye. If you do decide to make this ornament with candle wax then you will need to add your favorite color or scent and Stearine to your melted wax. Follow the instructions on how to add your dye and scent from the other projects in this book. You will need to insert a hole on the top of the ornament for hanging. When the ornament is finished you can warm up a wicking rod and insert a hole on the top of the ornament for adding string later for hanger. When the wax is fully melted pour the wax slowly into the mold. It helps to prop the candy mold inside a cup or container so that the wax can set up vertically. Set aside some of the melted wax for later if needed. Sometimes while the wax is cooling, the wax will create a dip on the top of the mold. Air bubbles cause this. Melt more beeswax and pour the melted wax into that area. Allow this to fully set up before attempting to remove the mold from the ornament.

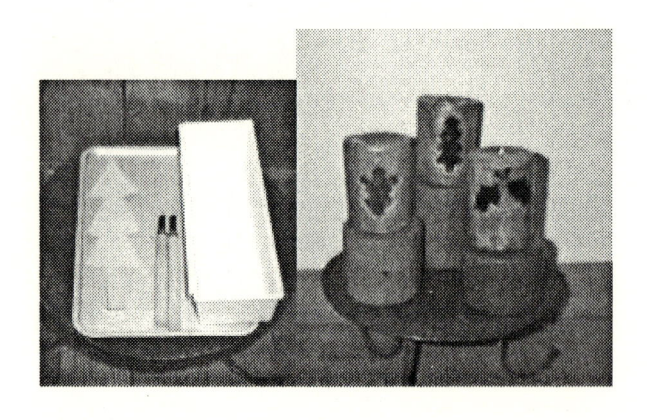

Carved Candles

Supplies needed:
- ✓ Beeswax/Candle wax (half of pound each) or
- ✓ Candle wax (one pound)
- ✓ Prepared wicks
- ✓ Stearine
- ✓ Candle dye
- ✓ Candle scent (beeswax has its own natural scent)
- ✓ Silverware drawer single compartment for mold
- ✓ Carving knife
- ✓ Template for your tree design
- ✓ Wicking rod
- ✓ Double boiler or electric frying pan and a can for melting wax

Please see the equipment and supply page for further instructions on how to prepare your wicks, what Stearine is used for, whether to use a double boiler or electric frying pan, and other tips you will need to know before you begin your projects.

First melt you Stearine at a low temperature. After the Stearine is melted then add your wax chunks and continue to melt at a low temperature. If you are going to make a beeswax candle base, then add half beeswax and half candle wax. While the wax is melting prepare your wicks. Soak your wicks into the melted wax for five minutes and remove to dry. If you are making a beeswax candle then you will not have to add any scent or dye. Beeswax has a natural scent and color. If you are making a candle from straight candle wax then you will need to add your dye and scent to the melted wax. A tip to check the shade is by dropping some dyed wax onto wax paper. If this is not the shade you want then just add more dye to the wax.

Prepare your mold by coating the inside lightly with vegetable oil. It is better to coat your mold just prior to pouring your wax so the oil doesn't dry. Coating your mold allows the wax to separate from the mold easier. You will need to make a template on paper for the design that you will carve into the top of your candle. I drew a basic tree. You can create your own design. Practice drawing different shapes and it is important to make sure the shape fits the top of your candle.

After the wax is fully melted pour the wax into your prepared mold. If you are making a candle from straight candle wax then you will need to add your scent to the melted wax. Allow this to partially set up and insert your wicking rod down the center for later placing your wicks. You will need to decide on how far apart and how many wicks you will need. I used three wicks two inches apart for my candle. Set aside a small amount of your wax and dye the wax the color you will want for your design. I choose green for my tree.

Allow the wax to set up for about thirty minutes and place your template, which you have made for your design, on the top of the candle. Score the design into the wax and carve away about 1/8 inches off the wax. Pour your melted wax into your scored area, allowing it to fully fill up your design. Allow the wax to set up for about ten minutes and lightly scrap off the layer of wax that is higher than your base candle. Scrap in a downward motion each time. When you are finished with scraping any excess wax off the top, then you will smooth the top wax of your candle with a hair blower. Place the hair blower directly above the top of your candle and warm the wax lightly the sides of the design flow into the base candle. The design you made should flow into your base candle. Use CAUTION and COMMON SENSE while warming your wax with a hair blower. Next run your candle under cold water and use a cotton ball to shine the wax. <u>Do not use your hair blower near running water.</u> <u>Safety always</u>!

Now you may place your wicks into the holes that you have previously made.

Antique Cookie Cutter Candle

Supplies needed:
- ✓ Beeswax/candle wax (half of pound each) or
- ✓ Candle wax (one pound)
- ✓ Candle scent (beeswax has its own natural scent)
- ✓ Candle dye (beeswax has its own natural color)
- ✓ Stearine
- ✓ Prepared wicks
- ✓ Wicking rod
- ✓ Double boiler or electric frying pan and a can to melt wax

Please see the equipment and supply page for further instructions on how to prepare your wicks, what Stearine is used for, how much candle dye and scent to use, whether to use a double boiler or electric frying

pan, and other tips you will need to know before you begin your project.

Prepare your cookie cutter by lightly coating the inside with vegetable oil. Seal the cookie cutter all around the edges with aluminum foil to prevent the wax from flowing out of the cookie cutter. You may also use putty to seal all around the cookie cutter, but make sure that the bottom is flat. This can be made into a candle and half candle wax. During this time prepare your wicks by soaking the wicks in the melted wax for five minutes. Remove the wicks from the wax and allow drying.

If you are not doing a beeswax candle then you will need to add your dye to your wax. A tip for checking the shade is by dropping some dyed wax onto wax paper. If this isn't the shade you want then add more dye to the wax. Repeat the first step. You will need to add scent to your candle wax after the wax is fully melted.

When the wax is fully melted pour the wax into your prepared cookie cutter.

After the wax is partially set up and has a cloudy appearance, insert the wicking rod down the center of the candle. Insert the prepared wick into the hole when the wax is fully set up. If you decide to use this as an ornament then you will need to prepare a hole on the top of the mold for hanging.

Remove the candle from your cookie cutter by tapping it lightly on the sides tipping the cookie cutter upside down. If you still have difficulties removing the candle then place it into the freezer for five minutes. This will allow the wax to shrink away from the mold.

Take the cookie cutter out of the freezer and run it under warm water. Your candle should slide right out of the cookie cutter.

These candles can be used as an ornament or a candle. If you do want to use it as an ornament then you will need to make a hole for hanging instead of for the wick. Use a pottery plate as a candleholder. Search around for a size that fits your candle. Always keep your eye out for different candleholders at flea markets or garage sales.

Floating Candle

Supplies needed:
- ✓ Candle wax (one pound of wax)
- ✓ Stearine
- ✓ Prepared candlewick
- ✓ Candle dye/blue
- ✓ Candle scent/blueberry
- ✓ Double boiler or electric frying pan and a can for melting wax
- ✓ Small muffin tin to be used for your mold
- ✓ Glass bowl to float your candle into

Please see the equipment and supply page for further instructions on how to prepare your wicks, what Stearine is used for, how much candle dye and candle scent to use, whether to use a double boiler or electric frying pan, and other tips you will need to know before you begin your project.

Prepare your muffin tin by coating the inside of each compartment with vegetable oil. This will aid you in removing the candle from your mold.

First you will need to melt your Stearine. This is melted before you add your wax chunks. Stearine helps the wax shrink from your molds for easier removal.

Then you will need to melt the wax in a pan at a low temperature. Never leaving wax unattended during melting time, as it is very flammable! Always melt your wax at a low temperature. While the wax is melting you can prepare your wick by soaking the wick for five minutes in the melted wax. Then remove the wick from the wax and allow drying.

When wax is melted completely add your candle dyes and scent according to amount you desire. One way to check the color is by dropping some colored wax on a sheet of wax paper checking to see if this is the color shade you wanted. Remember to allow time for the wax to cool to see the true finished shade. Remember the denser the wax the darker the shade. If not, then add more dyes to your wax and check again. Then gently stir the wax mixture. Wait until the wax is completely melted before you add your candle scent.

Pour your melted wax into the muffin tins slowly and allow to partially setup. When the wax has a cloudy consistency you will need to make the hole for the wick. Take your wicking rod and push it down the center of the candle. Sometimes during the cooling stage your candle will have a dip in the center. If this happens just add more melted wax to the candle. Allow the candles to setup fully before removing from the mold.

When the wax is fully setup you may remove the candles from the mold, tipping the pan upside down and lightly tapping the bottom of the pan does this. Now you will have to insert the wicking rod again down the center this time from the opposite side of the candle. The top of the candle that was seen from the muffin tin will now become the bottom of your candle. The last thing you will need to do is insert the prepared wick into the hole. Or if you prefer you can use the wider side for the wick, it works either way.

I used a glass bowl filled with water to float my candle. Add colored rocks on the bottom of the glass bowl to add more color to your candle decoration.

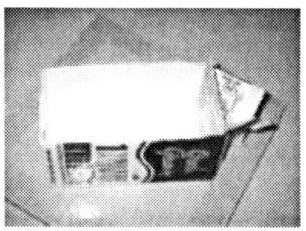

Cinnamon Rectangle Candle

Supplies needed:
- ✓ Candle wax (one pound)
- ✓ Stearine
- ✓ Prepared candle wick
- ✓ Double boiler or electric frying pan and a can for melting wax
- ✓ Candle dyes/red
- ✓ Candle scent/cinnamon
- ✓ 2-quart milk carton or 1-quart milk carton. (This depends on what size you want the finish product to be)

Please see the equipment and supply page for further instructions on how to prepare your wicks, what Stearine is used for, how much candle scent or candle dye to use, whether to use a double boiler or electric frying pan, and other tips you will need to know before you begin your project.

First add the correct amount of Stearine according to how much wax you will be melting. Melt this in your can at a low temperature.

Next melt the candle wax in a pan with the Stearine at a low temperature. This should be about 150 degrees. Remember wax is very flammable and you should never leave it unattended. When wax is melted completely you can add the dyes and scent. Add a small amount of candle dye first; you can always add more if needed. A tip to check the shade is by dropping some dyed wax onto wax paper. If this is not the shade you want then just add more dye to the melted wax.

Remember the denser the wax the darker the shade. Also you will need to add your candle scent to the melted wax.

While the wax is melting prepare the wicks. You can do this by soaking the wick into the melted wax for about 5 minutes. Then straighten and place the wick on wax paper allowing it to harden. Wicks should extend beyond the candle about one quarter inch. This is where you will have to decide how many wicks you will need. After the wax is fully melted add your candle scent.

Pour the wax into a milk carton that has been cut in half vertically (right through the middle) and positioned horizontally for a mold. Take a piece of the discarded carton and place it in the front of the end that is shaped like an angle. This will block the wax from filling into the angle, and the result will be a block shape end. Allow the wax to cool down slightly before pouring into the carton. To help prevent air bubbles in your wax pour the wax slowly. It is very common for your candle to end up with a dipped area in the center of the candle caused by the wax shrinking. Don't worry, just melt some more wax and fill it in. Set aside a small amount of your dyed wax for melting if needed later.

When the wax is partially set up insert your wicking rod through areas you will need to place your wicks. With a larger candle you will need to insert several wicks. This will aid the candle to burn evenly. I used three wicks and positioned the wicks about two inches apart.

You will need to wait until the candle is completely set up before you remove it from the milk carton. After you remove the candle from your mold insert your prepared wicks.

I used a metal plate stand as my candleholder that my husband made for me. You will need a large candleholder for this candle. Candleholders need to be larger than your finished candle to contain any wax that may drip while burning your candle.

Antique Rectangle Candle

Supplies needed:
- ✓ Beeswax/candle wax (half of pound each) or
- ✓ Candle wax (one pound)
- ✓ Stearine
- ✓ Prepared wicks
- ✓ Ground cinnamon
- ✓ Candle scent
- ✓ Candle dye
- ✓ Double boiler or electric frying pan and a can for melting wax
- ✓ Small loaf pan for a mold
- ✓ Wicking rod

Please see the equipment and supply page for further instructions on how to prepare your wicks, what Stearine is used for, whether to use a double boiler or

electric frying pan, and other tips you will need to know before you begin your project.

Prepare your loaf pan by lightly coating the inside with vegetable oil.

Melt your Stearine at a low temperature. Then add your chunks of wax and melt at a low temperature. When you are making beeswax candles use half beeswax and half candle wax, this will help the candle burn longer. Beeswax has its own natural color and scent so you will not need to add any additives like dyes or scents. If you are making this project with straight candle wax, then you will have to add candle dye and candle scent to the wax. A tip for checking the shade of your wax after adding the dye is by dropping wax onto wax paper. If this is not the shade you want then add more dye to the wax. Wait and add the candle scent to your wax when the wax is fully melted.

While the wax is melting you will need to begin to prepare your wicks. You may do this by soaking the wick into the melted wax for five minutes and then remove to dry. Depending on the size of your mold, you need to decide on how many wicks you will need for the candle to burn evenly. With this project I choose three wicks and spaced them evenly apart.

After the wax is fully melted pour the wax into your prepared mold slowly. By pouring the wax slowly you will prevent added air bubbles in the wax. This is where you will need to add your candle scent if you are making a candle made with straight candle wax. Sometimes during the cooling stage your candle with appear to have a dip on the top of your candle. Don't panic this is caused from air bubbles and the shrinking stage during the cooling stage. Just melt more wax and fill in the dipped area.

When the wax is partially set up, the wax will have a cloudy consistency. When this occurs you may insert the wicking rod into the areas you will need to place your wicks.

When the wax is fully set up you may remove the candle from the mold. Do not insert the wicks until after you antique the candle.

Now melt more candle wax and add your ground cinnamon until it is the shade you desire. Sprinkle more ground cinnamon onto the candle. Place a pan under the candle to catch the wax drippings. Insert the wicking rod into one of your holes that you made for your wicks to help hold the candle during this process. Pour the melted prepared wax over your candle. Repeat until you have acquired the shade you desire. Add your wicks by inserting the wicks into your prepared holes.

The candle in the picture is shown with a tray as a candleholder. I found this tray at a second hand store. Garage sales are another option for looking for unique candleholders. Be creative on how you want to display your candle!

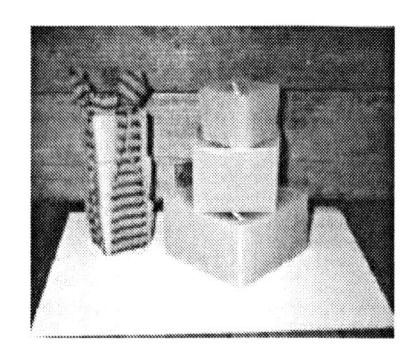

Square Candles

Supplies needed:
- ✓ Candle wax / beeswax (half of pound of each) or
- ✓ Candle wax (one pound)
- ✓ Stearine (not to be used with beeswax)
- ✓ Prepared candlewick
- ✓ Wicking rod
- ✓ Double boiler or electric frying pan and a can for melting wax
- ✓ Candle dyes
- ✓ Candle scents
- ✓ Milk cartons several sizes for molds/glass square candleholders three sizes

Please see the equipment and supply page for further instructions on how to prepare your wicks, what Stearine is used for, how much candle dye or candle scent to use, whether to use a double boiler or frying

pan, and other tips you will need to know before you begin your project.

When making a mold candle you will need to melt Stearine first before adding any wax. First melt the candle wax in a double boiler at a low temperature. Never leaving wax unattended during melting wax! If you are making a beeswax candle, then add half beeswax and half candle wax. You do not have to add any candle scent or candle dye to beeswax candles. Beeswax candles have there own natural color and aroma.

When wax is melted completely add the candle dye. A tip to check the shade is by dropping some dyed wax onto wax paper. If this is not the shade you want then just add more dye to the melted wax. Remember the denser the wax the darker the shade will become. Then gently stir the wax mixture. Pour the melted wax slowly into a milk carton. As the wax hardens you may see a dip form in the center. If this does happen pour more melted wax into that area. This is cause from air bubbles in the wax. Let the wax set up until it is cloudy and a thick consistency. Make an insertion in the middle of the candle for your wick. Let the wax set up completely. Now you may insert your prepared wick into the hole that you have previously made. Your wick size will change with the size of your mold. Follow the manufacture's suggestion on what size to use.

Candles Made From Old Tins

Supplies needed:
- ✓ Candle wax (one pound)
- ✓ Stearine
- ✓ Prepared wicks
- ✓ Old tins (various sizes and shapes)
- ✓ Double boiler or electric frying pan and a can for melting wax
- ✓ Candle dyes
- ✓ Candle scent
- ✓ Wicking rod

Please see the equipment and supply page for further instructions on how to prepare your wicks, how much candle dye and scent to use, what Stearine is used for, whether to use a double boiler or electric frying pan, and other tips you will need to know before you begin your project.

When you select your tin keep in mind that the base of the tin is larger than the top of the tin the candle will fall out with ease. Look at the inside of your tin to see if the top lip of your tin is rounded or not. If the lip is rounded then you will need to cut this edge away with a tin sniper. A rounded edge can prevent you from removing your candle from your mold. First melt the Stearine in your pan before you place your chunks of wax. Stearine is used to help the candle separate from the mold.

Next melt the candle wax at a low temperature. While the wax is melting add your candle dye. Stir the dye into the melting wax gently. Follow the manufacture instructions for the amount you need to use. A tip to check the color of the wax is to take a spoonful of colored wax and drop it onto wax paper to see if this is the right shade of color you wanted. If not, then just add more dyes to your wax. Remember to keep in mind that the thicker the wax layers the denser the color will become. Prepare your tin that you have chosen for your mold by lightly coating the interior with oil. This helps the wax from separating from the mold. At this time you should also prepare you wicks. This is done by soaking your wick in the melted wax for about 5 minutes and then take the wick out of the melted wax to dry on a piece of wax paper.

After the wax is completely melted pour the wax into the mold slowly. By pouring the wax slowly into the mold it may prevent some air bubbles from forming. After the wax is partially set up you may insert the wicking rod down the center of the candle. This will make your hole for the wick to be placed later. Depending on the size and diameter of your candle you may have to place several wicks into your candle. My mold was about 5-inch square, so I decided that I needed three wicks for this candle. If you are not sure on how many wicks to use, go look at the store for different dimensions of candles and see how many wicks they use.

Sometimes when the candle hardens in the center of the wax will appear a dip. Don't worry; this can be remedied easily by filling in more melted wax into that area. That is why I like to set aside some of my melted wax.

When the candle is fully set up, you may remove the candle from its mold. To do this just flip the molds upside down and lightly tap the bottom of the mold.

The candle should fall out with ease. If this doesn't happen then place the mold into the freezer for five minutes to help the wax shrink from the mold. Do not leave the candle in the freezer to long or it will begin to crack the wax. Place the wicks into the holes that you made.

Tins can be used as candle molds or use as a container candle. Pottery or tins plates make great candle holders, so keep an eye out for different and interesting shapes to use for future candles. Flea markets and Goodwill are great places to look for plates.

Variable Candle

Supplies needed:
- ✓ Candle wax (two pounds)
- ✓ Stearine
- ✓ Prepared candle wick
- ✓ Double boiler or electric frying pan and a can for melting wax
- ✓ Candle scent/citrus
- ✓ Candle dyes/yellow, red, and green
- ✓ Molds: old tins (various sizes and shapes), plastic cups (comes with egg coloring set)

Please see the equipment and supply page for further instructions on how to prepare your wicks, how much candle scent or dye to use, whether to use a double boiler or frying pan, what Stearine is used for, and other tips you will need to know before you begin your project.

First add the correct amount of Stearine, based on the amount of wax you will be melting, and melt this at a low temperature.

Next, you will need to cut your wax into chunks and place the chunks into your melting can. Melt the candle wax at a low temperature. Never leave the wax during melting time unattended, and always have adult supervision while making candles. When the wax is melted completely add the candle dye. A tip to check the color is dropping a small amount of colored wax on a sheet of wax paper to check the shade. If this is not the shade you desire then just add more dye to the melted wax. This is a multi-colored candle. I choose to use three colors, but you can use more if desired. Therefore I have three cans of wax melting; one can for each color.

Prepare you mold by coating the container or tin with a thin coat of vegetable oil. Be careful to not use too much oil in the mold or the oil will leave bubbles on the outside area of your candle. When choosing a mold for your projects, make sure that the top of the mold is the same size as the bottom of the mold.

Some tins will have a lip on the top that can prevent you from removing the candles. You can cut the lip with snipers.

While your wax is melting you may begin to prepare your wicks. To prepare your wick you soak the wicks in the melted wax for five minutes. After soaking the wick remove the wick and allow drying. This is where you will have to decide how many wicks you will need for this candle. The larger the diameter of the candle the more wicks you will need for the candle to burn evenly. For this candle I have choose three wicks and left two inches in between each wick. It may be helpful for you to visit a store that sells candles and familiarize yourself with their placements of wicks.

In order to achieve a wave design you will need to prop the tin in different directions for each layer. This decision should be made prior to pouring the melted wax into your mold. After the wax is fully melted I add my scent. You can choose to have several scents with each color or just use the same scent with all colors.

Pour a small amount of prepared wax into the mold, and then let this layer of wax set up for about twenty minutes before pouring the next layer. Continue with this process until the desired height is obtained. When you finished pouring the last layer, take your rod and insert through the middle of your candle to prepare for the wick hole. Let this candle set up fully, because shrinkage may occur. If this does happen, then just add more melted wax into the dipped area. Sometimes tapping the mold lightly will allow air to escape from the hot wax. Allow all layers of wax set up fully. Now just turn the mold over and lightly tap the bottom of your mold to help the candle fall out. Final step is to insert your prepared wicks into the holes you have made.

Be creative and make all different sizes, shapes, and color combinations for your variable candle. I've found that a pottery or tin plate used as a candleholder gives this variable candle a more rustic accent.

Container Candles

Supplies needed:
- ✓ Candle wax / beeswax / one pound of wax
- ✓ Prepared candlewick
- ✓ Wicking rod
- ✓ Double boiler or electric frying pan and a can for melting wax
- ✓ Canning jars; any interesting shaped glass container or tins
- ✓ Candle dye and scent

Please see the equipment and supply page for further instructions on how to prepare your wicks, how much candle scent or dye to use, whether to use a double boiler or electric frying pan, and other tips you will need to know before you begin your project.

First melt the candle wax in a pan at a low temperature. If you are making a beeswax candle the formula for the wax is half beeswax and half candle wax. You do not have to add candle scent and dye to beeswax candles, be cause they have their own natural scent and dye. If making a candle with straight candle wax then you will need to add candle scent and dye. When making a container candle you do not need to add any Stearine to your candle wax. Never leave your wax unattended while melting! To prepare your wicks soak the wick into the melted wax for five minutes and remove to dry.

While the wax is melting add your candle dye. A tip to check the shade is by dropping some dyed wax onto wax paper. If this is not the shade you want then just add more dye to the wax. After the wax is fully set up add your candle scent. Stir the scent in the wax gently. Now pour the wax into your container slowly to help prevent air bubbles.

When the wax is partially set up insert the wicking rod down the center of the candle for you wick. A dip might appear in the center of your candle during the cooling stage. If this happens just add more melted wax and fill in that area. Insert the wick in the hole that you previously made.

I always keep my eye out for interesting and different styles of containers, glass, or tins that can be used later for my candles. Check out those garages sales or your local Goodwill store. Be creative!

Cylinder Candles

Supplies needed:

- ✓ Beeswax/ Candle Wax (one half pound of each) or candle wax (one pound)
- ✓ Stearine (optional if using straight candle wax)
- ✓ Molds: frozen juice containers, small Pringles potato chip container, 5 oz. Dixie cups, or oatmeal container (cut to the desired height)
- ✓ Prepared wick
- ✓ Wicking rod
- ✓ Double boiler or electric frying pan and a can for melting wax

Please see the equipment and supply page for further instructions on how to prepare your wicks, whether to use a double boiler or electric frying pan, and other tips you will need to know before you begin your project.

First decided on what type of mold you will need. If you are using a mold that is glass, tin, or another hard surface, you should coat the mold lightly with oil. Oatmeal containers, Dixie cups, and other paper-based molds do not need any preparation. Whenever you make a candle with straight candle wax that requires a mold, you will need to add Stearine first to aid in removing the candle from the mold. Stearine will help shrink the wax during the cooling stage.

Begin to melt your wax, when making beeswax candle your formula for the wax is half beeswax and half candle wax, at a low temperature. Beeswax candles will have their own natural scent and color so adding any candle dye or candle scent is optional. But if you decide to make your cylinder candle from candle wax you will need to add scent and dye to your wax during the melting process.

When the wax is melted you can begin to prepare your wicks. To do this you will need to soak the wick into the melted wax for about 5 minutes, and then remove from the wax and allow drying. Remember the size of the wick is determined by the diameter of the candle.

Follow the manufacture instruction for the correct size.

After the wax is completely melted, pour the wax into the prepared mold slowly to prevent bubbles. When the wax is partially set up then insert the wicking rod down the center of the candle for later placement of the wick. The wax at this point will look cloudy and have a thicker appearance.

Sometimes when the candle hardens in the center of the candle a dip may occur. Don't worry; this can be remedied easily by filling in more melted wax into that concave area.

When the wax is fully set up remove it from the mold. Gently tapping the side of the mold and tipping it upside down allowing the candle to fall out can aid in removal. If you still have difficulty with removing the candle, put the mold into the freezer for about 5 minutes to help the wax shrink. Remove the mold from the freezer and run it under warm water. This usually does the trick. Never leave the candle in the freezer for longer than 5 minutes or it will cause the wax to crack. If you are using a cardboard mold then tear the cardboard away from the candle for removal.

Now you can insert the prepared wick into the hole that was made previously.

Any of these candles can be made with any color dye and your favorite candle scent. Experiment with your own ideas and creations.

I used a block of wood for my candleholder. Other options to use are pottery plate or folk art designed plate. Don't limit yourself to my suggestions, shop around and find that perfect looking candleholder. Maybe it is right in your cupboard!

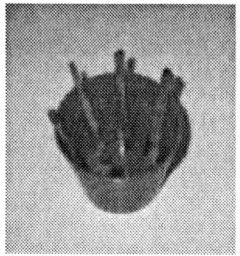

Beeswax Cinnamon Stick Candle

Supplies needed:
- ✓ Beeswax/candle wax (half of pound each)
- ✓ Prepared wick
- ✓ Plastic cup for a mold (I used a container that comes with a Easter dying kit)
- ✓ Cinnamon sticks
- ✓ Wicking rod
- ✓ Double boiler or electric frying pan and a can for melting wax

Please see the equipment and supply page for further instructions on how to prepare your wick, whether to use a double boiler or an electric frying pan, and tips you will need to know before you begin your projects.

To begin with you will need to prepare your mold by adding a light coat of oil to the inside of the mold. (You can use any vegetable oil for this procedure)

Take and cut into chunks one-half pound of beeswax and one half pound of candle wax. Melt your wax at a low temperature. While the wax is melting prepare the wick. Place the wick into the melted wax and soak for five minutes and then remove to dry. Dip each cinnamon stick in the melted wax, and then arrange each cinnamon stick upright periodically on the inside wall. This will secure the cinnamon sticks during the next step. Now slowly pour the remaining amount of wax into the mold leaving a top space so that the cinnamon sticks protrude out higher than the top layer of wax. Allow the wax to partially set until it appears to have a cloudy appearance.

When the wax is partially setup take the wicking rod, that has the same diameter or larger of the wick, and run it down through the middle of the candle leaving a hole that later you will insert the wick through.

Allow the wax to completely set up and turn the mold over tapping it lightly so the candle will slide out of the mold. If you still have difficulty in removing the candle from the mold you can place the mold into the freezer for about five minutes. After removing the mold from the freezer place the mold under warm water to help ease the candle from the mold. This will help the wax shrink from the sides of the mold. Do not leave the mold in the freezer longer because it will begin to crack the wax.

You will now need to insert the wick into the hole that you made earlier. This method seems to make a straighter hole for your wick placement.

A great additive to give with this candle gift is a jar of honey. Your Beeswax cinnamon candle will give off a natural honey aroma which will aid to the cinnamon smell.

Whipped Candle

Supplies needed:
- ✓ Candle wax (one pound)
- ✓ Stearine
- ✓ Prepared wicks
- ✓ Cylinder shape mold (salmon can works well for this)
- ✓ Bowl for whipping the wax/fork or spoon to whip the wax
- ✓ Candle scent/blueberry
- ✓ Candle dye/blue
- ✓ Wicking rod
- ✓ Double boiler pan or electric frying pans and a can for melting wax

Please see the equipment and supply page for further instructions on how to prepare your wicks, how much candle dye and scent to use, whether to use a double boiler or electric frying pan, and other tips you will need to know before you begin your project.

You will need to make a base candle first for this candle project.

Melt the Stearine at a low temperature. This will help your wax shrink away from your mold. I used a salmon can for my mold, but you can use any size can for your base mold. Prepare your mold, if using a can, by coating the inside lightly with vegetable oil.

Next you will need to melt your candle wax at a low temperature. While the wax is melting you may add your candle dye. I used blue candle dye with this project, but you may should your favorite color for this candle. Add a small amount of candle dye first because you can add more if needed. A tip to check the shade is by dropping some dyed wax onto wax paper. If this is not the shade you want then just add more dye to the wax. Remember the denser the wax the denser the color will become.

Prepare your wick during the melting stage. To prepare your wick soak the wick into the melted wax for about 5 minutes allowing it to harden on a sheet of wax paper. I prefer to add my candle scent to the wax when it is fully melted and I have removed the can from the pan. Experiment on how much scent to use!

When the wax is fully melted you may pour the wax into your mold. Allow the wax to partially set up before you make the hole for your wick. I like to wait until the wax is thicker and has a cloudy appearance. Do not insert your wick into the base candle until you have added the whipped layer of wax.

Sometimes when the candle hardens a dip will appear in the center of the candle. Don't worry, you will be adding your whipped wax all around the base and this will fill in the dipped area.

After the candle is fully set up you may remove the candle from the mold. To do this you will simply turn the mold upside down and lightly tap the bottom of the mold. If you have difficulty with this procedure then place the mold into the freezer for about five minutes to help the wax shrink away from the mold. Do not leave the candle in the freezer to long, because the wax will begin to crack. Now you are ready to do the next step of this candle.

Melt more wax with the same amount of candle dye slowly at a low temperature. Pour the wax into a glass bow and quickly begin to whip the wax. Please wear safety glasses during this stage to prevent any wax from splattering into your eyes. Safety is a must at all times while making candles. I used an aluminum pan under my bowl to protect my working area from hot wax. When clumps begin to form in your melted wax then quickly place the base candle into the bowl. Spoon the wax around the base candle to add an even layer of whipped wax. If your wax sets up before you are finished with the whipped layer of wax, melt the wax over and repeat this step. Make sure to keep your wick hole clear. You may have to insert the wicking rod down the center again. Now you may insert the prepared wick.

A tin or pottery plate works well for a candleholder. Dried berries or flowers can be placed around the plate to give the candle a more country look.

Cinnamon Apple Candle

Supplies needed:
- ✓ 2 quart milk carton
- ✓ Candle wax (one pound)
- ✓ Candle dye/green
- ✓ Ground cinnamon
- ✓ Small votive glass for your center candle
- ✓ Prepared wick
- ✓ Wicking rod
- ✓ Double boiler or electric frying pan and a can for melting wax

Please see the equipment and supply page for further instructions on how to prepare your wicks, what Stearine is used for, whether to use a double boiler or electric frying pan, and other tips you will need to know before you begin your project.

First you will need to make a votive candle for your center apple scented candle. Cut your wax into chunks and melt it at a low temperature. Never leave your melting wax unattended. Wax is very flammable. While the wax is melting prepare your wick. Soak the wick into the melted wax for five minutes and remove to dry. Now add your candle dye. A tip to check the shade is by dropping some dyed wax onto wax paper. If this is not the shade you want then just add more dye to the melted wax. Remember the denser the wax the darker the shade. When the wax is fully melted add your candle scent. After the wax is partly set up and has a cloudy appearance then insert the wicking rod down the center for your wick hole. Now you have made your green apple center candle.

Melt your remaining candle wax at a low temperature. When the wax is fully melted add enough ground cinnamon to give your candle a dark cinnamon appearance. Lightly whip the cinnamon wax until the wax has a cloudy consistency. Wear safety glass to protect your eyes during the whipping process. Place your votive candle in the center of the carton. Begin to slowly pour the cinnamon wax into the carton filling all around the glass candle. Let this set up completely and then tear away the mild carton from around the wax.

I used a green tray that I found at a second hand store for my candleholder. Place dried apples around the base of the candle to add some more green color to your candle.

Give this candle as a gift with added fresh apples. The fresh cinnamon scent combines nicely with the apple scent to give this candle an interesting aroma.

Oatmeal and Honey Candle

Supplies needed:
- ✓ Beeswax/candle wax (half of pound each)
- ✓ Candle wax (half of pound)
- ✓ Stearine
- ✓ Candle scent/vanilla
- ✓ 2 quart milk carton
- ✓ Small votive glass for base candle
- ✓ Prepared wick
- ✓ Wicking rod
- ✓ ½ cup of oatmeal flakes
- ✓ Bowl to whip your wax into
- ✓ Double boiler or electric frying pan and a can to heat wax

Please see the equipment and supply page for further instructions on how to prepare your wicks, what Stearine is used for, whether to use a double boiler or

electric frying pan, and other tips you will need to know before you begin your project.

Place your glass votive inside the oatmeal container sure there is enough space around the glass for your wax base, and then cut the container according to the height of your glass votive for your candle. When I look for a votive glass for this type of project I will choose a glass that can be easily removed after the candle burns down. You will need to have a glass where the sides are straight or the base is smaller than the top. If the base is larger than the top you will not be able to remove the candle from the base.

You will need to make your base candle first.. Melt half beeswax and half candle wax together at a low temperature. Beeswax or container candles do not need any Stearine added to the wax. <u>Never</u> leave your wax unattended during the melting stage.

While the wax is melting you will need to prepare your wick for your base candle. Take and soak your wick into the wax for five minutes and remove to dry. After the wax is fully melted begin to slowly pour the wax into your votive glass. When the wax is partially set up insert the wicking rod down the center of the candle for the wick hole. Sometimes during the cooling stage the wax will shrink and form a dip in the center. This is cause from air bubbles. Don't panic and just fill in more melted wax into that area. That is why I keep aside some of my wax just for this. Place the wick into the hole after the wax fully set up.

Next you will need to melt your wax for the base. Melt your chunks of candle wax at a low temperature. When the wax is fully melted add your vanilla scent to the wax. Pour the melted wax into a bowl and begin to whip your wax until it becomes thicker in consistency. Add about ½ cup of oatmeal flakes to your wax. Make sure your oatmeal container is cut to the height you want and have the votive glass place in the center of the candle. Quickly pour the oatmeal wax around the center candle. Add more oatmeal flakes to the top of the base. Allow to fully set up before you remove the container from the wax.

Give a jar of honey with your candle as a gift. I painted a small plate a honey color to use as my candleholder. A bottom of a terra cotta pot works well as a base for your candle. Add a bee to the top of your candle for that *country look*.

Egg Shaped Candle

Supplies needed:
- ✓ Candle wax (one pound)
- ✓ Prepared candlewick
- ✓ Double boiler or electric frying pan and a can for melting wax
- ✓ Candle dyes/purple
- ✓ Candle scents/lavender
- ✓ Empty eggshells for mold

Please see the equipment and supply page for further instructions on how to prepare your wicks, how much candle dye and scent to use, what Stearine is used for, whether to use a double boiler or electric frying pan, and other tips you will need to know before you begin your project.

First cut an opening out of the top of an eggshell. The smaller the opening the more of the natural shape you will be able to keep intact. You will probably have to practice with a few eggshells first. Then empty the egg out of the shell and let it dry. This will be your mold for the egg candle. You can lightly coat the inside of the eggshell with oil to aid the wax from separating from the eggshell.

Melt your candle wax chunks in a pan at a low temperature. Never leaving wax unattended during melting time, as it is very flammable!

When your candle wax is melted completely, add your candle dye. A tip to check the color is by dropping some colored wax on a wax paper until you produce the desired color needed. Remember the denser the wax the darker the shade. Melt your candle wax at a low temperature, around 150 degrees. After the wax is melted, I add scent to the wax.

Pour the wax into your eggshell slowly to help prevent added air bubbles. Let the wax partially set up in the eggshell before you gently insert the wicking rod down the center of the candle. Set aside some of your melted wax for later, just in case you will have to use it to fill in the dip made during the cooling stage. During the cooling stage the wax will shrink and leave a dip.

Be creative and make all different colored egg candles. You can make an layered egg candle by pouring one colored wax into the egg shell – let it set up for about one half hour and then add another layer or however many layers you prefer.

When the wax is fully set up, insert the wick into the prepared hole and remove the eggshell from the candle. The eggshell will remove easily in some areas, but other areas it may remove piece by piece – just take your time!

Pinecone Fire Starters

Supplies needed:
- ✓ Candle wax
- ✓ Candle dye (I used red)
- ✓ Candle scent (I used cranberry)
- ✓ Wicking rod
- ✓ Prepared candlewicks
- ✓ Double boiler or electric frying pan and a can for melting wax
- ✓ Pinecones (large)

Please see the equipment and supply page for further instructions on how to prepare your wicks, what Stearine is used for, how much candle dye and scent to use, whether to use a double boiler or electric frying pan, and other tips you will need to know before you begin your project.

First melt you wax at a low temperature, never leave melting wax unattended! Wax is very flammable!

When the wax is melted completely, add your candle dye. A tip to check the shade is by dropping some dyed wax on wax paper. If this is not the shade you want then just add some more dye to the wax. Remember the denser the wax the darker the shade. Then gently stir the melted wax.
Prepare your wick the same as the other candle projects.

When the wax is fully melted remove the wax from the heat. Add your candle scent to the melted wax. There isn't any magic formula on how much scent to use. Your sense of smell will determine how much you want to use.

Begin dipping the pinecones into the can of melted wax slowly. Repeat the dipping process until you have acquired the amount of layers of wax you desire. Cut a small wick and attach the prepared wick under one peddle of the pinecone.

Remember these are to be used for fire starters only! Pinecones with the combination of wax are very flammable!

Please give *instructions* on how to properly to use these fire starters! Clearly state that these are not *candles* they are *fire starters for a fireplace.*

I like to package six to nine fire starters in a gift box.

Lemon Citronella Candle

Supplies needed:
- ✓ Candle wax (one pound)
- ✓ Wicking rod
- ✓ Prepared wicks
- ✓ Clay pot for candleholder   (I seal the clay pot with paint or varnish so the wax will not soak through the pot)
- ✓ Double boiler or electric frying pan and a can for melting wax
- ✓ Candle dye (yellow)
- ✓ Citronella oil/lemon candle scent

Please see the equipment and supply page for further instructions on how to prepare your wicks, what Stearine is used for, how much candle dye and scent to use, whether to use a double boiler or electric frying

pan, and other tips you will need to know before you begin your project.

First melt your candle wax chunks at a low temperature. Never leave your melting wax unattended! Wax is very <u>flammable</u>!

Prepare your wicks. There are instructions on the wick package for what size wick to use verses diameter of the candle.

Now you may add your dye to your melted wax. I chose yellow for my candle to go with my lemon scent. Stir the wax gently to mix the dyes completely. A tip to check the shade is by dripping some dyed wax on wax paper. If this is not the shade you want then just add some more dye to the wax. Remember the denser the wax the darker the shade.

When the wax is completely melted, remove the wax from the heat before adding your candle scent and citronella (follow the instructions that came with your scents on how much to use). Pour your wax into your clay pot slowly. Set aside a small amount of wax for later usage. During the cooling stage your wax may form a dip in the center of your container. This is normal and happens from the air bubbles that form during the melting process.

When the wax is cooled and has a cloudy appearance, insert your wicking rod down the center of the wick. A wicking rod is any metal rod approximately the diameter of your wick. You may need to use more than one wick depending on the diameter of you pot. The instructions on the wick package will give you an idea on what size wick to use according to the diameter of your pot. When the wax is fully set up insert your prepared wick.

There are several types and sizes of clay pots. Some clay pots have a baked or painted outer covering on it. You can use a plain clay pot and decorate the pot with acrylic paint.

Bowl Candles

Supplies needed:

- ✓ Bowl shape candleholder
- ✓ Vaseline
- ✓ Aluminum foil
- ✓ Stearine
- ✓ Candle wax (one pound)
- ✓ Candle scent (apple)
- ✓ Candle dye (green)
- ✓ Prepared wicks (#3)
- ✓ Double boiler or electric frying pan and a can to melt wax
- ✓ Plaster for mold (box patching plaster is sold in any hardware store)
- ✓ Plaster coated gauze for final mold

Please see the equipment and supply page for further instructions on how to prepare your wicks, what

Stearine is used for, whether to use a double boiler or electric frying pan, and other tips you will need to know before you begin your project.

Step one/ bowl shape: prepare the inside of your candleholder that you have chosen for this project by coating the inside with aluminum foil (smooth out the foil to form the bowl shape). Follow the directions for preparing the plaster, and then pour it into your candleholder. Allow the plaster to fully set up (this may take several days depending upon how much plaster it took to fill the bowl. When the plaster is fully set up, remove the plaster mold from the bowl.

Step two/Mold for wax: Coat the bottom of the plaster with Vaseline so that you will be able to separate the two molds from each other. Mix the plaster gauze accordingly to the directions, and begin layering the gauze on the bottom of the bowl covering the whole area with several layers. Allow this to set up until fully dried, and then separate the two molds. This mold can be used again for your next candle.

Step three: Prepare your wicks by soaking the wick into the melted wax for five minutes and remove to dry.

Step four: Melt the precut chunks of wax, adding the correct amount of Stearine at a low temperature. Add the green candle dye and stir into the wax gently dispersing the dye evenly. A tip to check the shade is by dropping some dyed wax onto wax paper. If this is not the shade you desire then just add more dye to the wax.

Step five: After the wax is fully melted add your candle scent. Stir the scent in the wax gently. Pour the prepared wax into your mold. When the wax is partially set up, insert the wicking rod into the designed areas for your wicks. (How many wicks you choose will depend on the diameter of the candle) The wax will appear to be cloudy. Insert the wick in the hole that you have provided after the wax is fully set up. Sometimes after the wax has cooled a dip will appear in the center of the candle, just add more melted wax to the dipped area.

Luminaries

Supplies needed:

- ✓ Luminary Candleholder
- ✓ Prepared container candle or votive candle
- ✓ White sand
- ✓ Hammer and punch tool (for homemade tin can luminary)
- ✓ Tin can (if you are making your own luminary)

Please see the instruction page for preparing your container candle for this project. I like to use a small container for luminaries; a baby food jar works great.

After you prepare your container candle (see instructions for container candles) the most difficult part of this project is choosing the luminary to fit your occasion. I like using baby food jars for my luminary containers because they are small enough size for most containers. Look around in your cupboards or refrigerator for any small glass jars that can be used for your container candle and don't throw away the lid. The lid will help keep the wick from getting dusty when your candle is not being used.

Votive candles work well inside a luminary container. (See instructions for votive candles) If you place a votive candle in a glass jar without sand your candle may tip and the flame can cause the jar to break. So it is very important to use sand on the bottom of your luminary bag or container pressing the candle into the sand to stabilize it.

There are many choices you may use for a luminary, a metal luminary that you have purchased from a store, a paper bag luminary (please buy the bags that are made for luminaries because they are flame retardant), a homemade tin can luminary, or a cheese grater luminary. Be creative and come up with your own idea on what to use for your special luminary. Always be cautious on where you place any candle, and remember to put the candle out.

If you are using a cheese grater for your luminary, please keep in mind when removing the grater; it can be hot on top.

A tin can luminary is very easy to construct. Choose a tin that the side ridges are not too close together (this will enable your design to stand our more in-between the ridges). Make a pattern by wrapping a piece of paper around the can. Lay paper on a flat surface, and then draw your pattern on the paper with a series of dots. Just like the dot-to-dot pattern you connected as a child. Set the pattern aside until later. Then place water into the tin can to about ¼ of inch below the top rim of the can. Place the can into the freezer to begin the freezing process. After the water is frozen, tape the pre-made pattern around the can. Use your punch tool and hammer to pound the holes from your pattern until the design is complete. Keep in mind the size of your hole will determine the amount of light your luminary will omit. Allow the reminder of ice to thaw, and dry your tin can.

To create a freehand design, use regular crayon to draw a pattern onto the tin then rub it off prior to painting. If you are not comfortable with a freehand design, then trace a pattern to your can. Paint your design with metal paint found at craft stores.

Luminaries are a great decoration to light up your sidewalk, or just to light up your favorite room in your house. *Caution and common sense* is always needed whenever you have any candle lit in your house. Never place a candle on a surface without added protection from the heat omitted from a burning candle.

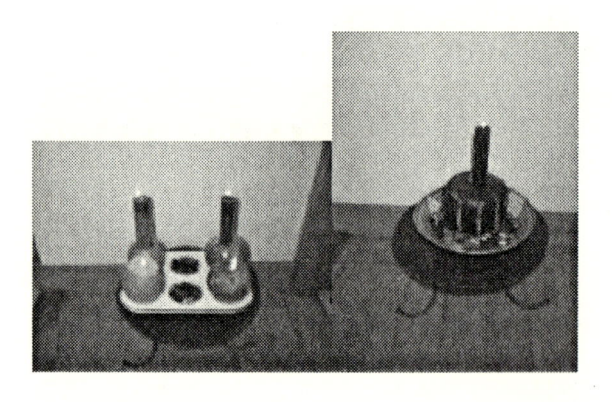

Fruit Candleholder

Supplies needed:
- ✓ Prepared tube or votive candle
- ✓ Apple, orange, squash, or pumpkin
- ✓ Tray, plate, or muffin tin to place your fruit candle into

Please see instructions for tube or votive candle to use for your Fruit candle holder.

Dig out an area in the center of the fruit of your choice large enough to place a tube candle, or a small votive candle inside. The choice of fruit that you will use will depend on the season or holiday. I always place all of my candles on some type of a plate or tray to protect the area from melting wax, or to aid in preventing the candle from tipping. I listed just a few choices of a fruit or vegetables that can be used on your table, but be creative and come up with a choice of your own.

You're not limited to a tube or votive candle with this project. Another choice you may use is melting wax directly in the center of your fruit or vegetable. For this choice you can go to the instructions for a container candle and use the fruit or vegetable as your container. If you opt for melting the wax directly into the fruit, remember that you need to do this right before you intend to use this candleholder as your table arrangement. Fruit will only stay fresh for a short time.

For added decoration around your fruit or vegetable candle, a smaller fruit like cranberries or grapes give this table decoration more color. Do not use any type of dried leaves, dried grass, potpourri, or beads close to the candle. This can catch on fire cause by melting wax.

Frequently Asked Questions

Q: I have been trying to make heavily scented candles, but they do not fill the room or even the air above the candle. Do you have a suggestion on supplier and amount of scent used?
A: On my web page I have a suggestion on a supplier that I use. A different manufacture produces different qualities in scents. You will have to shop around. First try the manufacture suggestions on amount to use, but if this doesn't satisfy you then experiment on different amounts. The trick I have found is that you add the scent last after the wax is melted, colored, and cooled several minutes. I like to smell the scent as I add it to the melted wax. Adding the scent last keeps the scent from evaporating away versus adding the scent during the heating process. Always use scents that are made for candle wax.

Q: Do you have suggestions for Vybar/Stearic acid?
A: Vybar and Stearic acid are used for the same thing. This is to make your wax more opaque and harder. For mold candles Stearic acid aids in shrinking the wax, result will separate from the mold easier. Vybar is used with rubber and copper molds because Stearic acid is a caustic. Generally rule of

thumb is: 9 part wax to 1 part Stearic acid. Again my suggestion is to follow the manufacture suggestion of amount to be used. It is very important to weigh your wax so that you can you the correct amounts of dyes, scents, and Stearic acid to your wax. You will need to melt the Stearic acid before you add your wax chunks for melting.

Q: Can you use paraffin wax for candle making?
Yes paraffin wax will work fine for candle wax. Candle wax is a paraffin base with a small amount of Stearic acid added to the wax. Paraffin wax can be easily found in the canning department of most stores.

Q: I am interested in using dried fruits... apples and oranges etc. Can you offer any advice to begin?
A: Whenever you use any dried herbs, fruits, flowers, or beans always use caution! Adding dried items to your candle can aid in the appearance of your candle, but when burnt can leave off a burnt aroma during the burning process. If you burn your candle down to far this can make your candle more flammable! You can use herbs for a natural scent and drain the herb over cheesecloth to remove the herb. I like using a glass container for my center candle and then add the dried substance to the wax that

surrounds the center candle. This way I am assured that my candle with not catch on fire from my added dry substance. Experiment with your candle that you make in a safe environment while burning that new project. Safety always first!

Q: How can I get started making candles?
A: Begin first with a simple project. Votive candle using Dixie cups for your molds is a good beginner project. This will allow you to get the feel of melting wax, adding dyes and scents, and using the correct size of wicks for your candle. First research where you will be able to get your supplies, and begin to collect all the equipment you will need to begin making candles with. Go to stores and look at different styles, colors, and scents used in candles. This is a good opportunity to look at how many wicks they use for different diameters and lengths of their candles. Think simple and as you get more comfortable with this project then work on a more difficult project.

Q: What type of wax do you need to carve with?
A: Paraffin or candle wax will work out great. I worked for years in a Dental Laboratory and we begin

our dentures with wax, adding layers and smoothing the wax around the straight edges. First decide what you want to carve, and draw out a pattern. What shape are you making? What size will this be? Would it be better to start with a base size candle and add to that base? What will you use for your base candle? Keep some melted wax going on a low temperature to add slowly for layers. A heated spoon will work for smoothing out those rough edges. I suggest in one of my projects to warm your wax with a blow dryer. After adding layers, while the wax is still warm lay your template on the area to be carved and begin to carve away that shape. If you don't like your finished project then melt it and start all over again. That is the beauty with this craft.

Q: *What can I use for molds?*
Anything and everything almost! Look around your house for containers, glasses, plastic cups, can from food products like tuna or tomato paste, paper juice containers, milk or juice cartons, or metal and plastic pipes. I can go on and on, now you need to use your imagination. Remember if you use a can, the inside of the can should be smooth for removal. If you use a tin container the bottom should be larger or the same size as the top for removal. Dixie cups (various sizes)

not only work well as a mold, but also can be used to store that leftover wax from your projects. Flea markets, Goodwill Stores, and garage sales are great places to shop for molds or containers for your candles.

Q: *Can you make molds from plaster?*
A: Yes, this will be where your creativity and imagination will play a part with candle making. Again working in a Dental Laboratory we used plaster to make our molds. We coated the plaster with Vaseline to help the wax from separating or soaking into the plaster mold. First decide what shape you are making, and always draw out a pattern. You can buy plaster at any store in small amounts. There will be instructions on mixing plaster. Use cold water with mixing with plaster so you will have more time before the plaster sets up. Plaster can be carved and smooth out easily when it is still soft. Wet your fingers and smooth the edges of the plaster. You can shape plaster around any object, but you will need to remember that it must separate from that object after it sets up.

Q: *Can you make old beeswax candles look shiny again?*

A: Use an old nylon sock or any nylon material and rub lightly on the candle to regain its shine. Beeswax will bloom with age.

Q: *Can you make your own mold from metal?*
A: If you are handy with soldering and have access to metal, yes! Take time and draw out your pattern and cut it out for a template. After you cut your pieces out solder the sides together. You can also make interesting metal candleholders. Take a piece of metal and cut it into a plate shape and crimp the edges.

Q: *What temperature should you melt candles at?*
A: General rule is 130 – 150 degrees F. Always heat wax at a low temperature. Wax is very flammable so never leave the melted wax unattended! This is a project that should only be done with adult supervision!

Q: *What can I use for molds?*
A: Just about anything you can get your hands on! Juice containers, tuna cans, plastic cups, Dixie cups, old tins, metal or plastic piping, and muffin tins. I can go on and on! Look around your house and see

what you have in your cupboards. You will find that you won't throw anything out.

Q: *Can I buy supplies online?*
A: There are several supplies online that will provide you with everything that you can use. Shop around and find the best prices. They will also have 800 numbers for you to call your orders in.

Q: *What type of containers do you use for your container candles?*
A: My favorite is old interesting shaped glasses, or canning jars. But the ideas on what to use are endless. Go to garage sales, Goodwill Stores, flea markets, or just check out your cupboards for mismatched juice glasses.

Q: *How do you place your wick in your candles?*
A: This was my frustrating part of making candles. Then I came up with the idea of using a wicking rod to produce a straight hole to place my wicks. My husband took welding rod the diameter of my wick and bent the end of it for a handle. I have used metal knitting needles also. Keep in mind you want this to be as close to the diameter of your wick as possible. When the wax is still warm but milky in color I insert

the rod where I want to place my wick, and then insert the wick into that hole. It works like a charm!

Q: What size wick do I use?
A: This depends on the diameter of your candle or the length of your candle. When you purchase your wicks they will give you a suggestion of size to use. If you are making a long candle then you may have to place several wicks for your candle to burn evenly. Go to the store and look at different types of candles and see how many or where they place their wicks. For a long candle I would place a wick every two inches.

Sometimes you will need to make your candle and burn it to see if the wick will burn evenly, or if the wick will burn out to quickly. If the wicks fall over into the pool of melted wax then maybe you should have used a wire core wick. If it only burns with a small pool of melted wax not filling up the whole candle, then you wick is too small. But if you put to large of a wick into a container it can crack your glass from too much heat. Practice makes perfect!

Q: Will beeswax burn well in a container candle?

A: Yes, but I still use the formula of half beeswax and half candle wax. Stearic acid is not needed for container candles.

Q: *Is there a homemade ingredient that I can use for scenting my candle?*
A: Yes, herbs, or flowers can be used in your melted wax to scent the wax. You can strain out the dried ingredient by placing cheesecloth over a pan to strain this out. If you want you may leave the dried ingredients in your wax, but beware that this may cause the candle to have a burnt scent. Also this can make your candle become more flammable. When I add anything to my wax that is dried I make a center container candle and then add wax around my glass container with my dried ingredients. Then there is no worry if the dried ingredient will catch on fire. Be careful with what you add to your wax!

Q: *When I make dipped candles the outside edge is bumpy!*
A: This is due to the dipping process of dipping into the melted wax and then dipping into water to cool the wax. Just take the candle and roll it lightly on a flat surface and the lumps will disappear.

Q: *I have a two-quart juice carton and don't know what to do with the folded edge.*

A: Cut away the top part of the carton for pouring the wax into, and then cut a small amount of this for adding to the v-shape end. This will make that end flat like the opposite end. Seal around the opening of your new wall with warm wax or putty. This also will make that wall more secure. Now you will have four 45-degree corners.

Q: *How do you get wax out of clothing?*

A: Use a piece of plain paper bag, and place it over the area that has wax on it. Then with a warm iron place the iron directly on that spot. Repeat this method, always with a clean piece of paper bag. Then all that is left is the oil from the wax. Spot this with some dish detergent to cut that oil stain.

Q: *Should I save my old pieces of candles? How do you clean the wax out of the container candles?*

A: I always save all my old pieces of candles and melt them with my new projects. Heat your containers in a pan of water until the wax melts out of the containers and wipe with paper toweling. I have an old pan that I keep just for this project.

Q: What should I do with the extra melted wax from my project?

A: Dixie cups work great for this job. Just pour the extra wax into Dixie cups for easy storage.

Printed in the United States
19679LVS00001B/100